BEST OF
RESTAURANT DESIGN

D0004305

BRAUN

BEST OF
RESTAURANT DESIGN

Imprint
The Deutsche Nationalbibliothek lists this publication in the Deutsche Nationalbibliografie;
detailed bibliographical data are available on the internet at http://dnb.d-nb.de.

ISBN 978-3-03768-056-8
© 2010 Braun Publishing AG
www.braun-publishing.ch

2nd edition 2010

Editorial staff: Annika Schulz
Translation: Stephen Roche, Hamburg
Graphic concept: Michaela Prinz

Preface

This volume brings together 42 exclusively designed restaurants, whose guests are assured not only epicurean delights, but satisfaction for all the senses. Indeed, France's first great restaurateur, Antoine Beauvilliers, who opened his Grande Taverne de Londres in Paris in 1782 and later revealed his secrets in the volume "L' Art du cuisinier" (which remains a standard reference work on haute cuisine), emphasized the importance of not only serving food and drink in the correct order, but also of creating the right spatial environment for fine dining. One of Beauvilliers' most frequent patrons was the famous gastronome Jean-Anthelme Brillat-Savarin. In his book, "The Physiology of Taste", this early restaurant critic confirmed that the Grande Taverne de Londres successfully united the key requirements of fine dining: an elegant setting, friendly service, a well-maintained wine cellar and outstanding cuisine. Brillat-Savarin deliberately mentioned the elegant surroundings first.

The restaurants featured in this book represent a global smorgasbord of interior design possibilities. They are located in cities as far apart as New York, London, Melbourne, Shanghai, Paris or Berlin, to name but a few of the cities represented. No less varied than the menus are the design concepts that have shaped these spaces. In recent years restaurants have found themselves competing with the new domestic dining room, which has arrived in many private residences due to the space-creating fusion of dining room and kitchen. These new living and eating spaces increasingly act as venues for

social functions or large dinner parties. What strategies have designers and architects come up with to counter this trend and enhance the restaurant's position as the main venue for public and social eating? One noticeable trend is the strict division of kitchen and dining area. The practice of integrating the cooking function into the restaurant experience as a form of spectacle – with food prepared at the table or the chefs' work made visible through a glass partition – seems to have passed. Instead, certain elements have been adopted from the domestic sphere, though employed in altered or amplified ways, such as a golden mirror mounted on the ceiling (Bella Italia, Stuttgart) or deliberately homelike lighting fixtures (Canteen, London und Tantris, Munich).

One trend that is noticeable in many newly-designed restaurants is a certain separation, a compartmentalization even, into individual tables for four or six guests. This creates private dining niches, almost private spaces that are separated from the rest of the room using a variety of materials; curtains, half-height wooden partitions, translucent layers, structured plastic ornamentation or organically shaped walls – whatever the imagination can envision. This basic concept of separating diners is in direct opposition to that of democratic dining. In restaurants where the democratic principle is applied all of the tables look the same, and often long, covered banquet tables or wooden boards are used. Restaurants like these do not have a 'best table in the house' (that might be adorned with a 'reserved' sign for a well-known patron). In such restaurants the idea is that the variety of the menu compensates for the lack of variety in seating arrangements. Despite the simplicity of the seating plan, many of these restaurants, which see themselves in the tradition of public canteens or eating houses, nevertheless experiment with design, particularly in terms of the materials used. As a result, a room that appears functional at first, where guests are served breakfast in rapid rotation, is transformed into a space that invites patrons to relax and take time with their meal. Perhaps the most essentially democratic of all seating arrangements – the round table of Arthurian legend at which all places are equal – is too closely associated with the dining habits of the middle ages. In any case, round tables are rarely to be found. Nowadays we tend to dine at rectangular tables, the longer the better, gathering around the banquet table like Leonardo's apostles at the last supper.

Here again the varied palette of materials that modern architecture uses is on display. In recent years the borders have once again shifted in the use of form, so that certain furniture designs that would have been technically impossible a few years ago are now a reality (Georges, Paris und Morimoto, Philadelphia). Yet much as some designers strive to produce eccentric and outlandish effects, others distinguish themselves by a reduction to the essential, for example by the restraining use of the color white (Isola Bar & Grill, Hong Kong, Olivomare, London or Schneeweiß, Berlin). In such restaurants a red wine spillage immediately assumes the status of an aesthetic disaster. Unfortunately it is not possible for us to gauge the extent to which interior design influences the menu or the vintages of the wines on offer. You will simply have to do the testing – and the tasting – yourself. Bon appétit!

Adour Alain Ducase | New York | Rockwell Architecture

This **design plays** with the **old** and **the new**

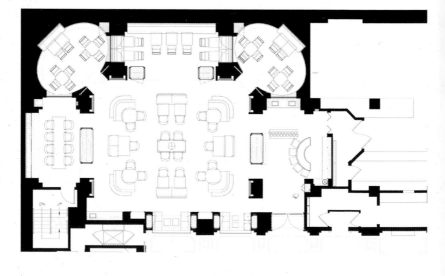

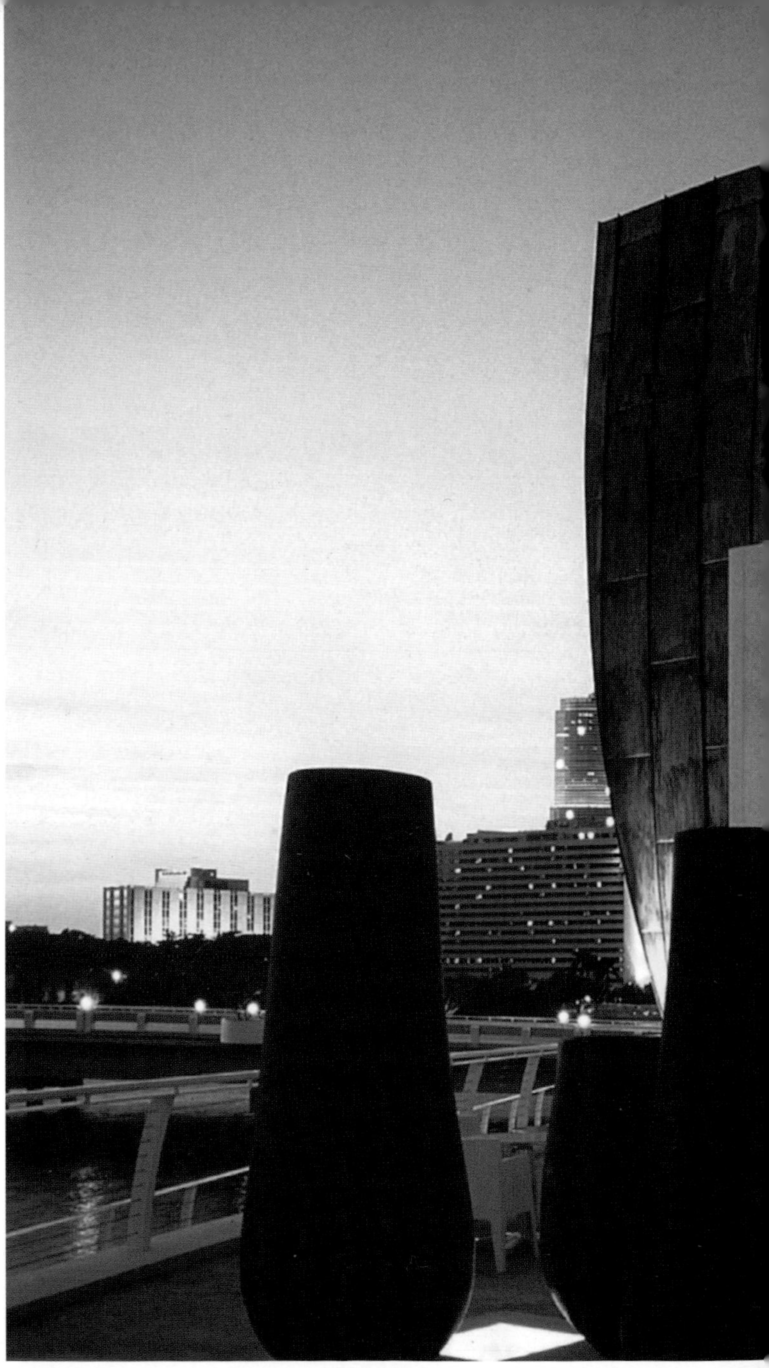

This **design** uses **dark wood,**
white marble surfaces
and seats of **woven rawhide**

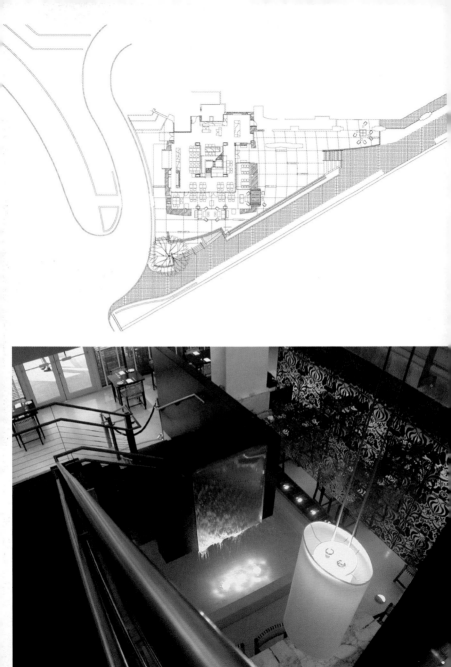

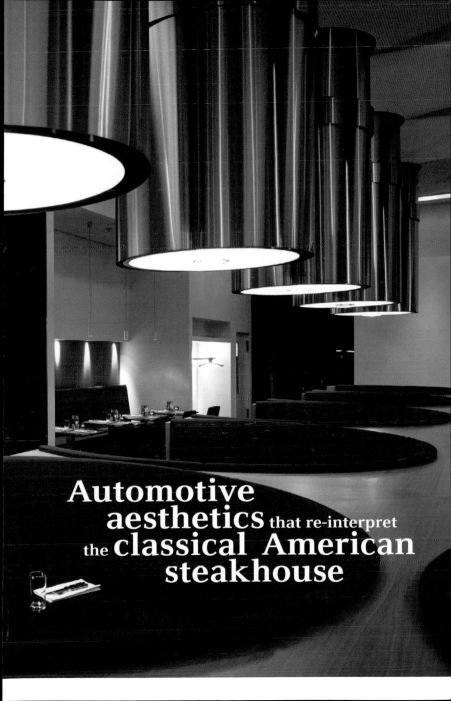

Automotive aesthetics that re-interpret the **classical American steakhouse**

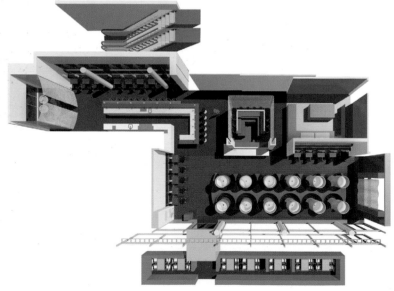

Furnishing and **materials** create a homelike **sitting-room** with an **informal** atmosphere

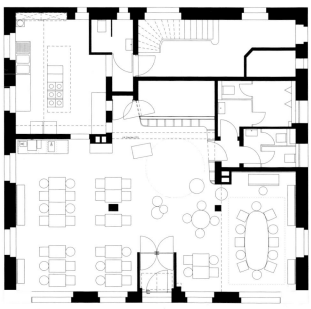

46 | **Bellevue** | Ittingen | Pia Schmid Architektur & Designbüro

Old and new elements in a multi-level setting

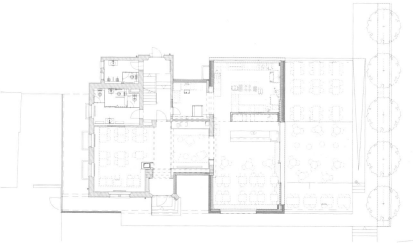

56 | **Buson Buffett** | Haeundae-gu, Busan | Studio Gaia

Dining booths are distributed **throughout** the restaurant to **break up** the symmetry and monotony **of the space**

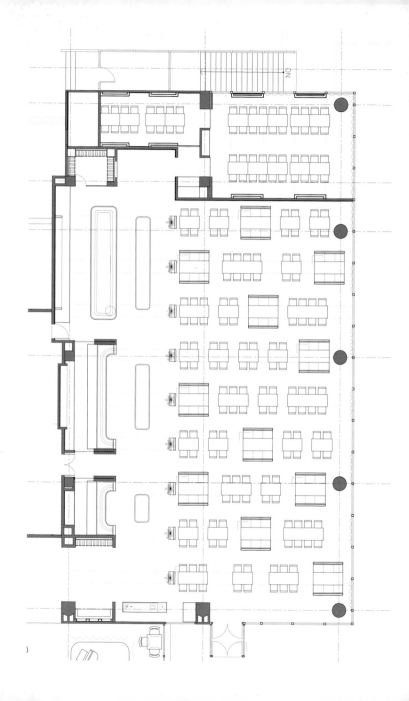

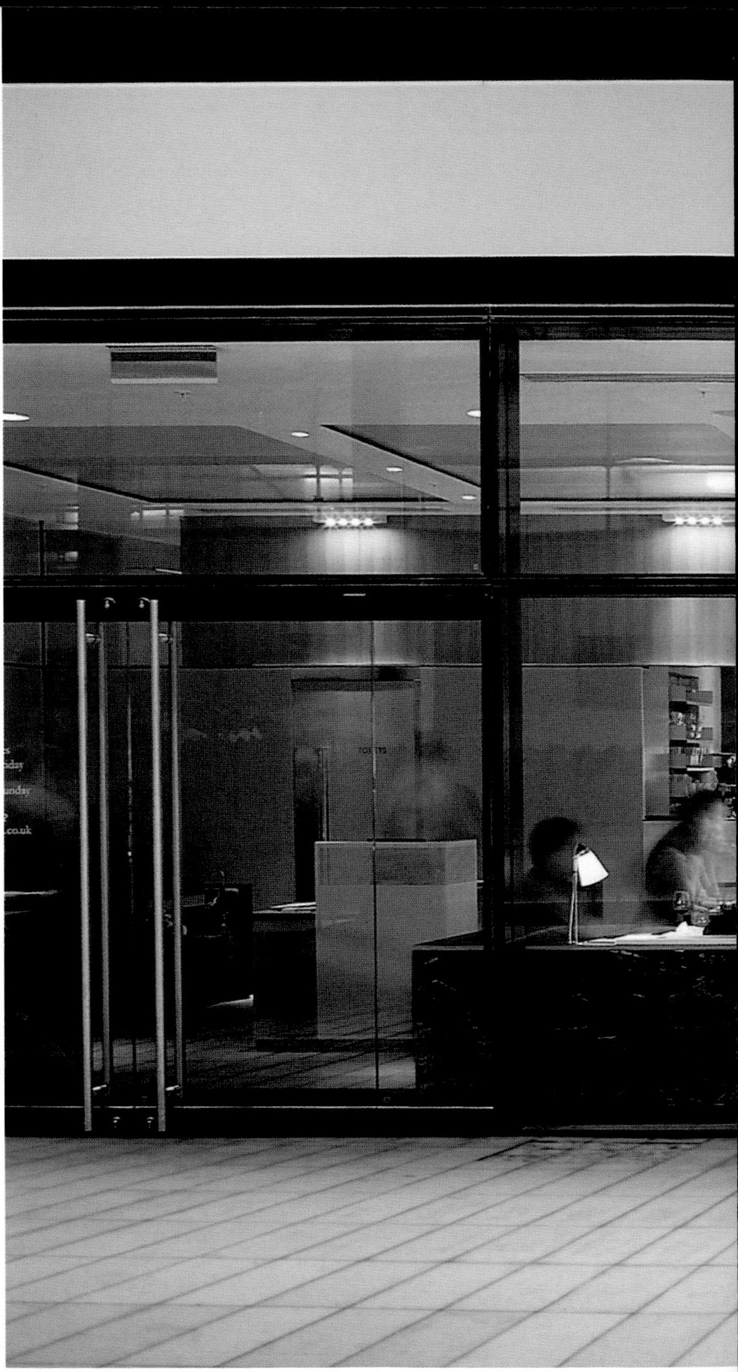

CANTEEN

Modern **British food** is reflected in **interior materials** and a spatial reference to **democratic dining spaces**

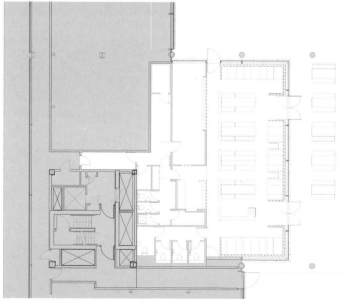

| **Casino Baden** | Baden | BEHF Ebner Hasenauer Ferenczy

Colorful **floral patterns** and **translucent curtains** create a modern **atmosphere**

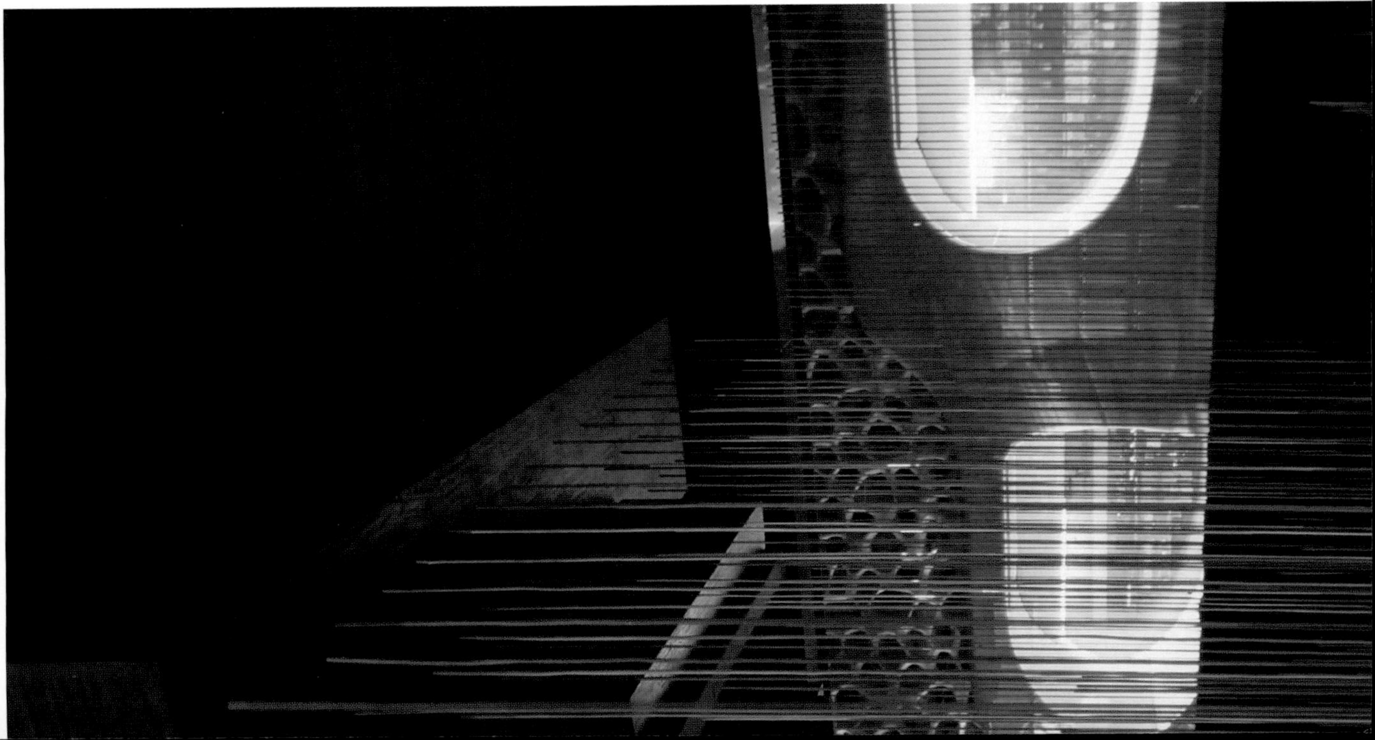

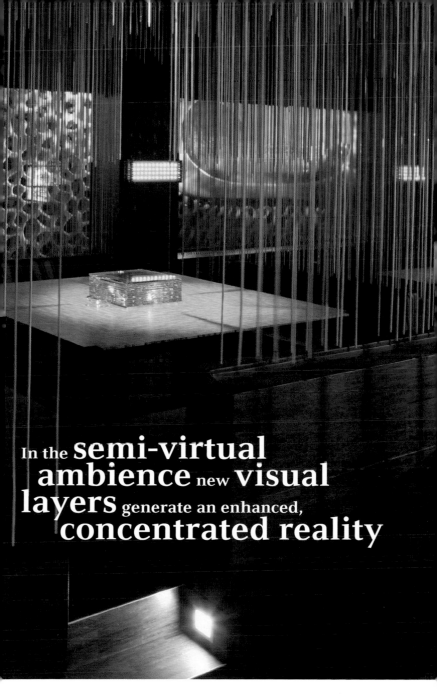

In the **semi-virtual ambience** new **visual layers** generate an enhanced, **concentrated reality**

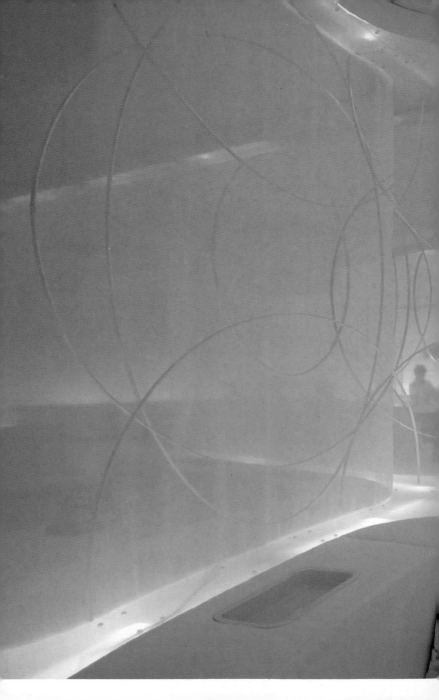

A simple yet **rich interior**
with a limited palette of
bronze, walnut, steel
and **leather**

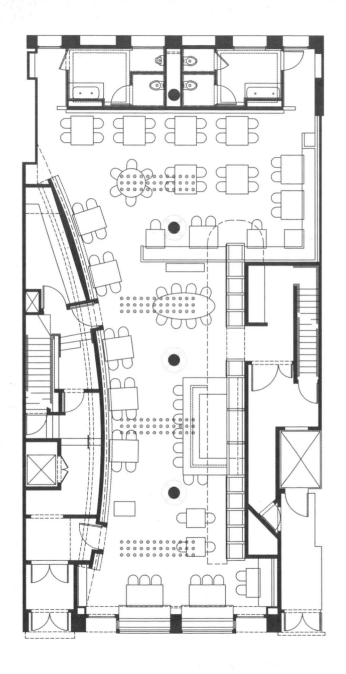

| **Danbo Fun** | Shanghai | MoHen Design International | Hank M. Chao

The **vinyl floor** tiles with **optical arts** patterns reinforce the **visual impact** of the **yolk**

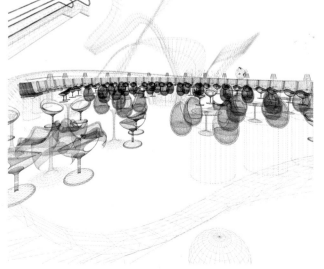

Basic essentials
like the **chandelier**
make this **place special**

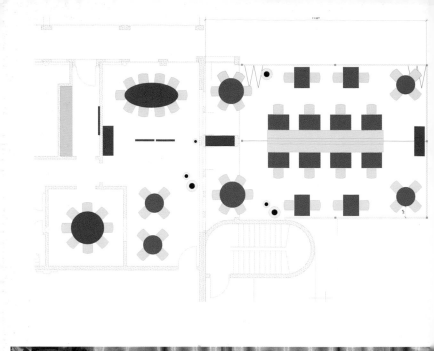

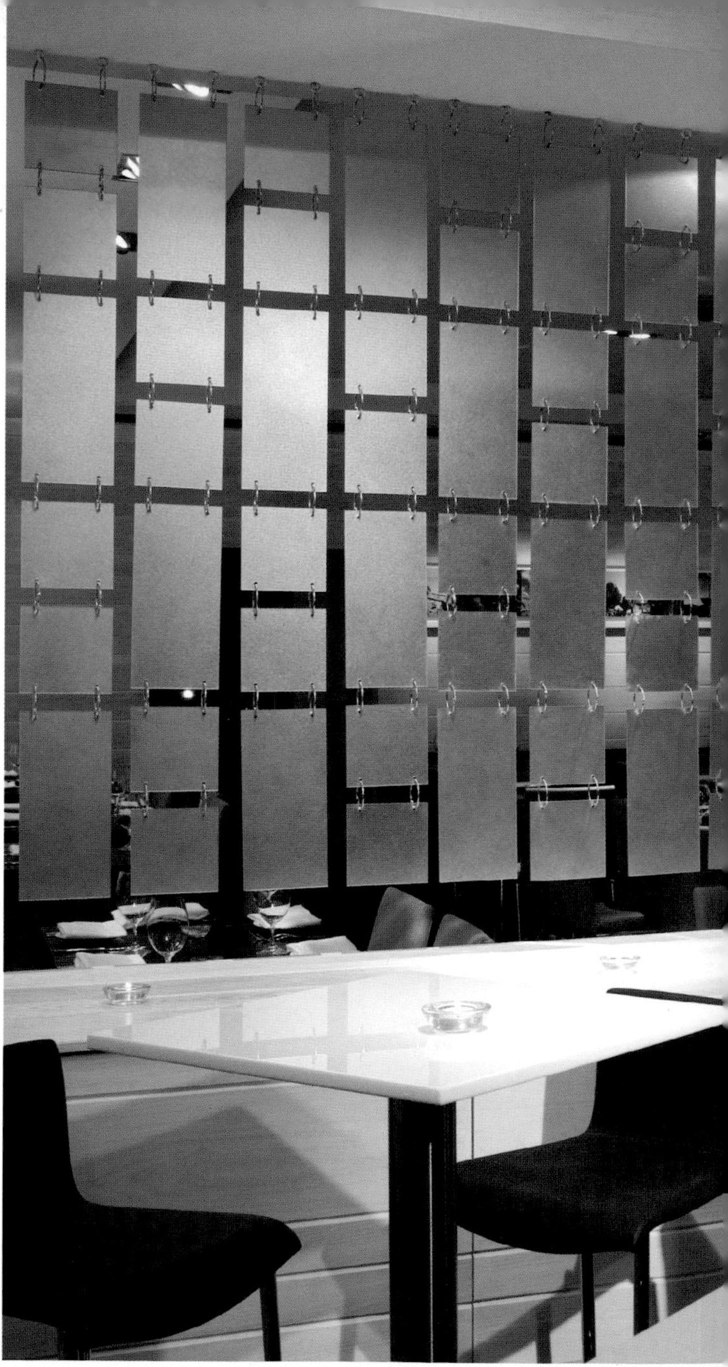

Designed to create an elegant yet casual dining experience, inspired by the cuisine

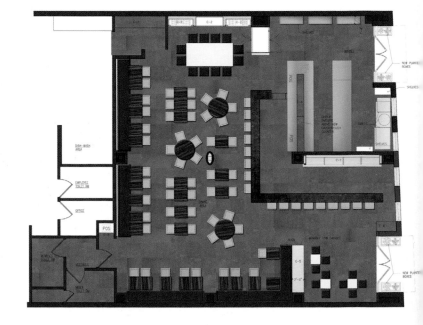

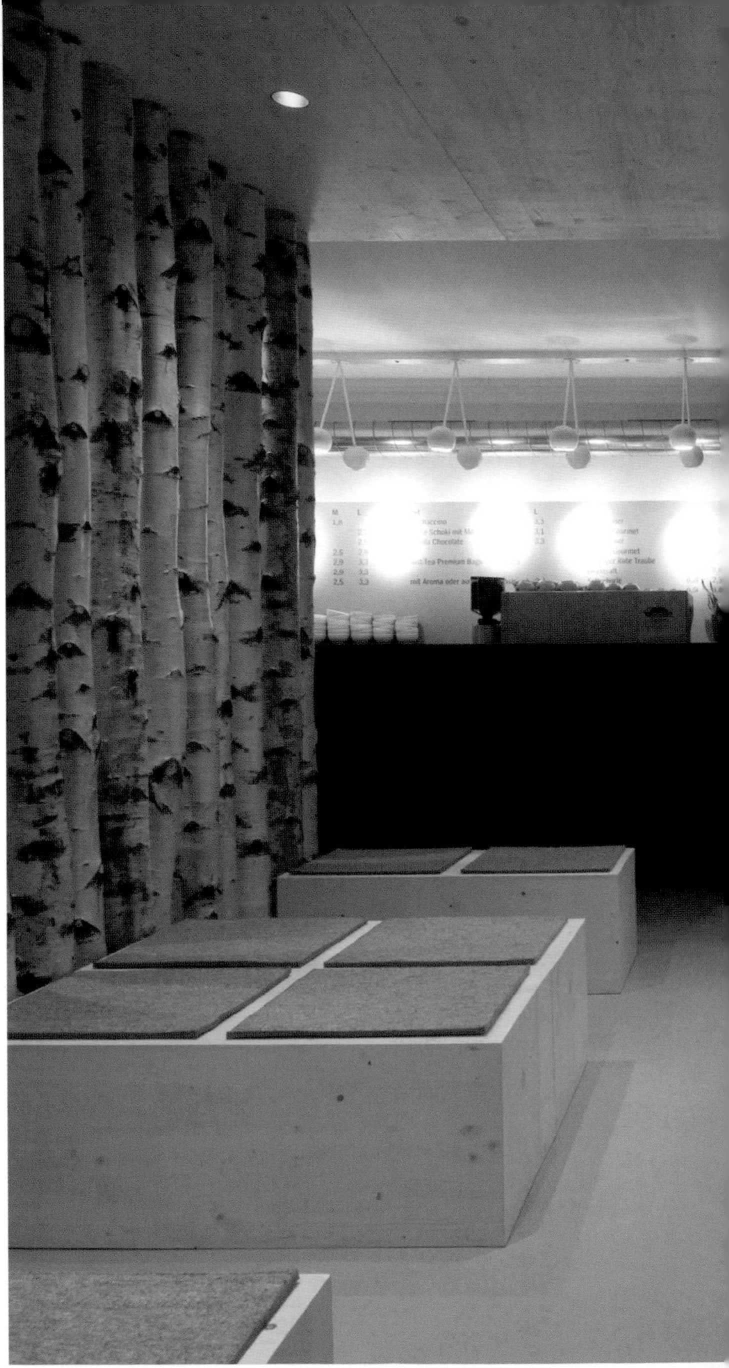

Birch logs act both as **opaque** room dividers and **symbols** of nature

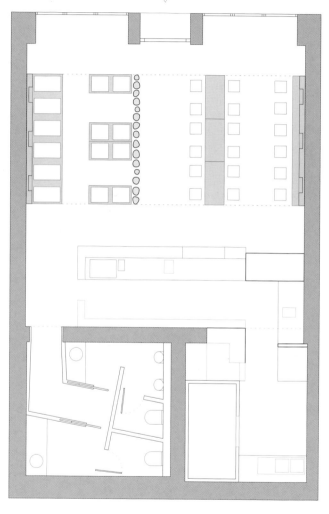

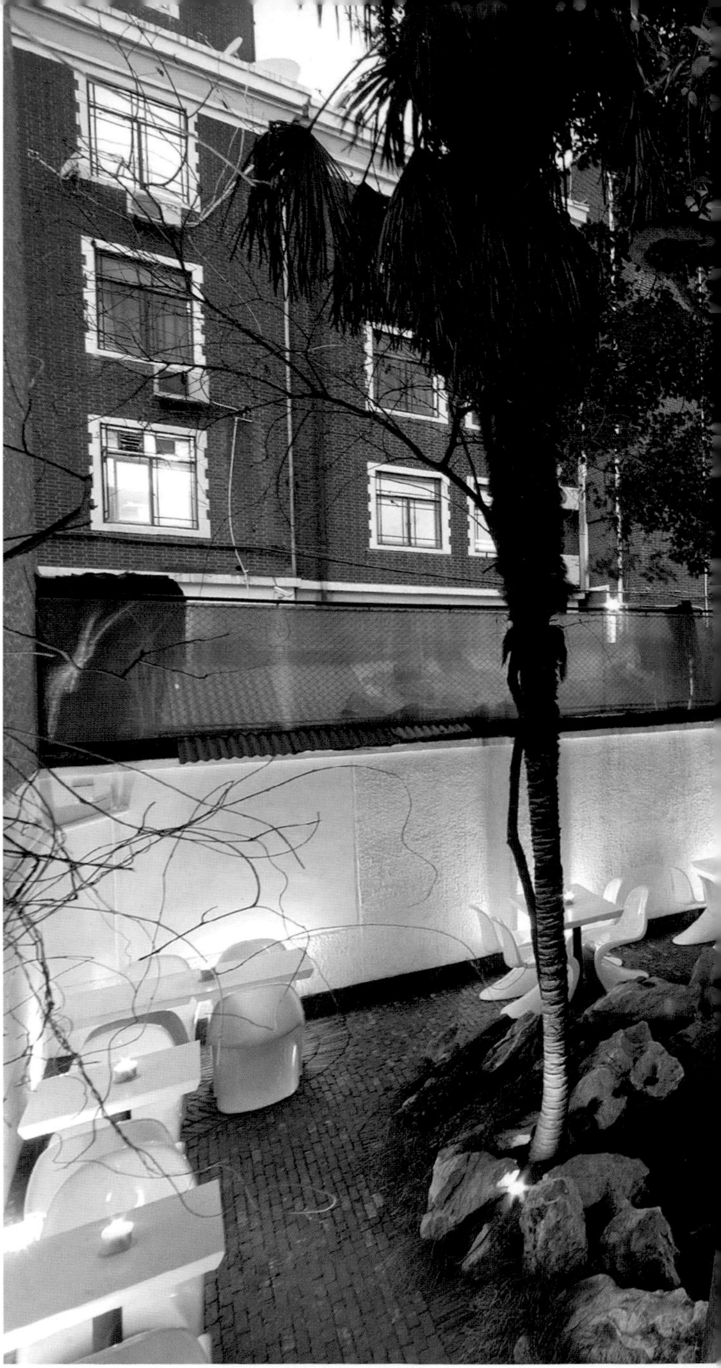

This is **where lifestyle** comes **to life**

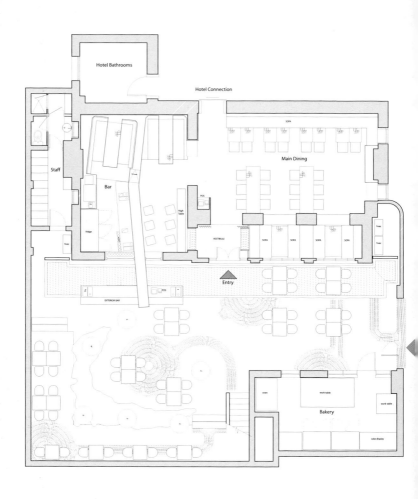

Hotel Bathrooms

Hotel Connection

Staff

Bar

Main Dining

POS

High
Table

VESTIBULE

SOFA

Entry

POS

EXTERIOR BAR

oven

work table

work table

Bakery

cake display

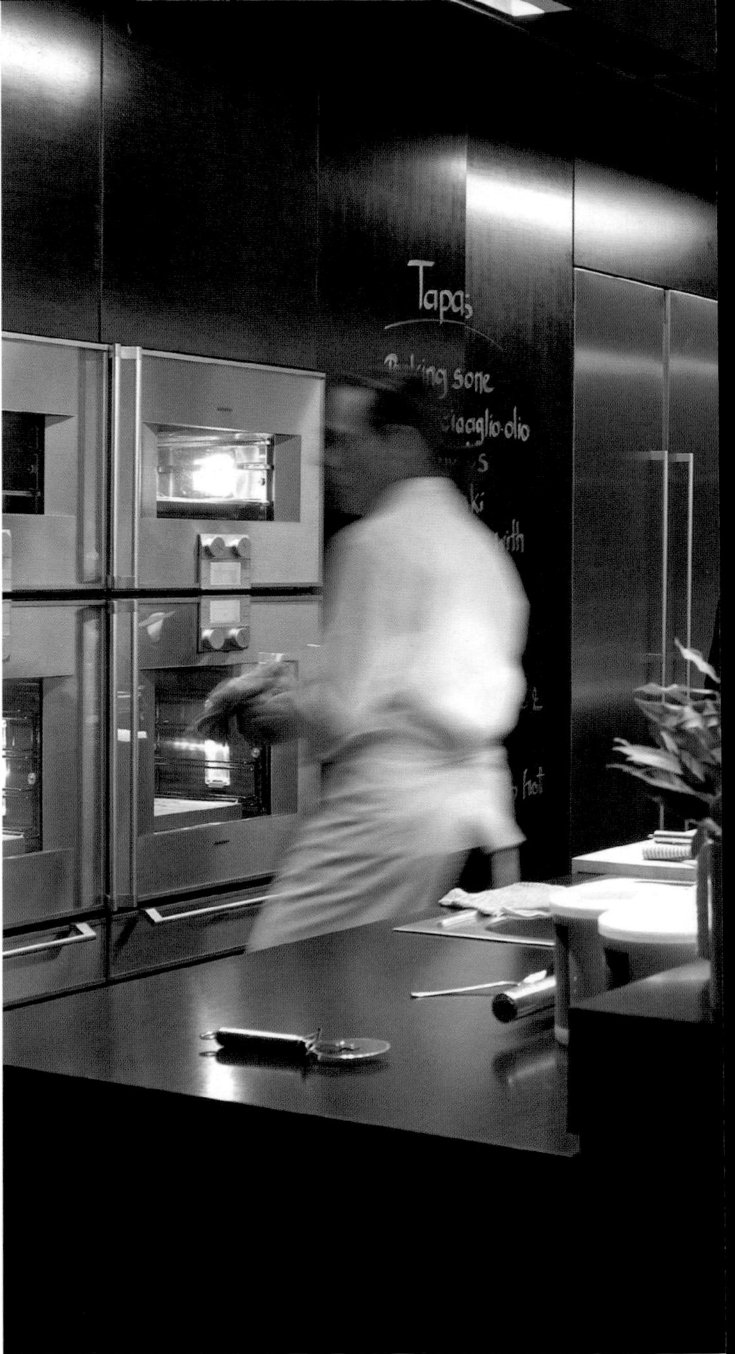
Tapas

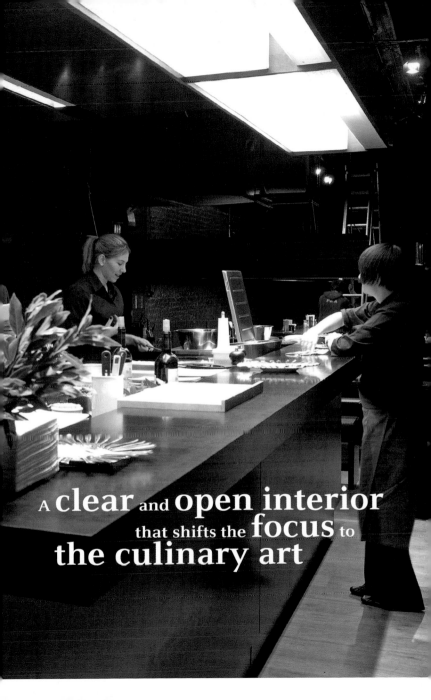

A **clear** and **open interior** that shifts the **focus** to the culinary art

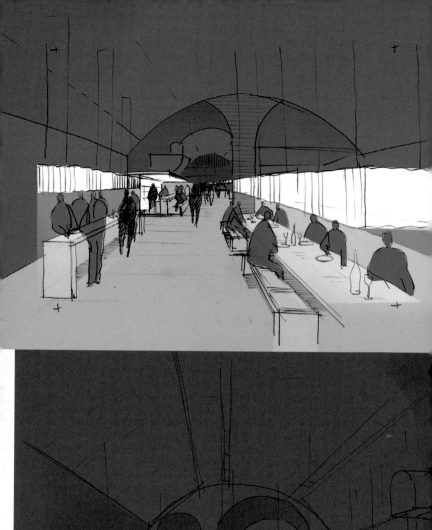
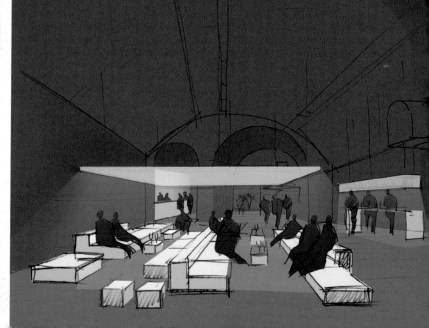

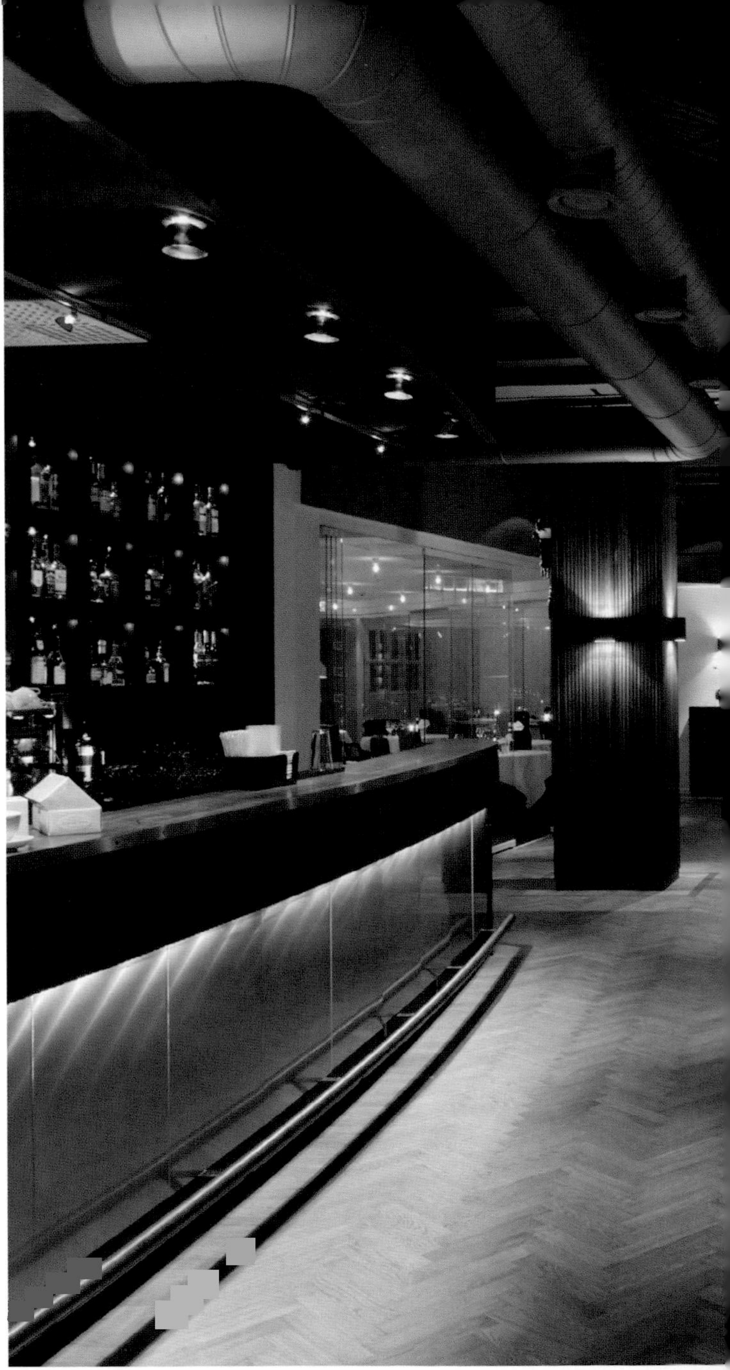

Sliding doors divide the classical and modern dining zones

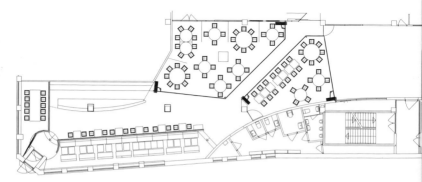

174 | **Georges** | Paris | Jakob + MacFarlane

Creating **new landscape camouflaged** interiors and **exteriors**

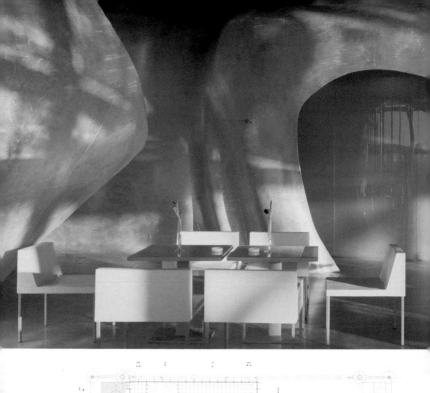

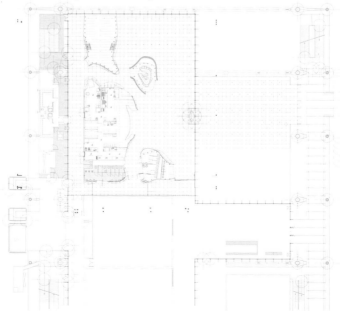

The **design draws** on traditional **Asian materials** with **walls** lined with **dark bamboo** poles

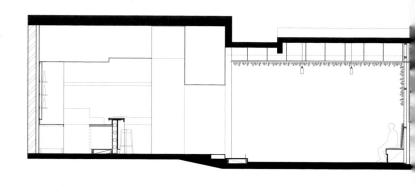

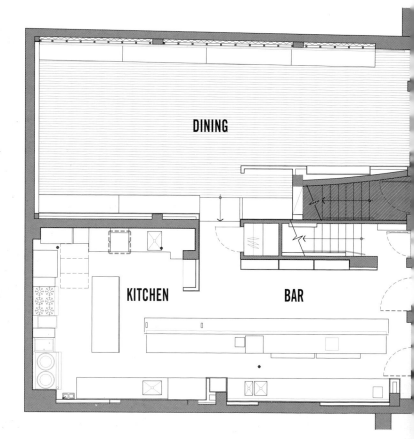

DINING

KITCHEN

BAR

An **earth palette** of **fabrics** and **furniture** grounds the **restaurant**

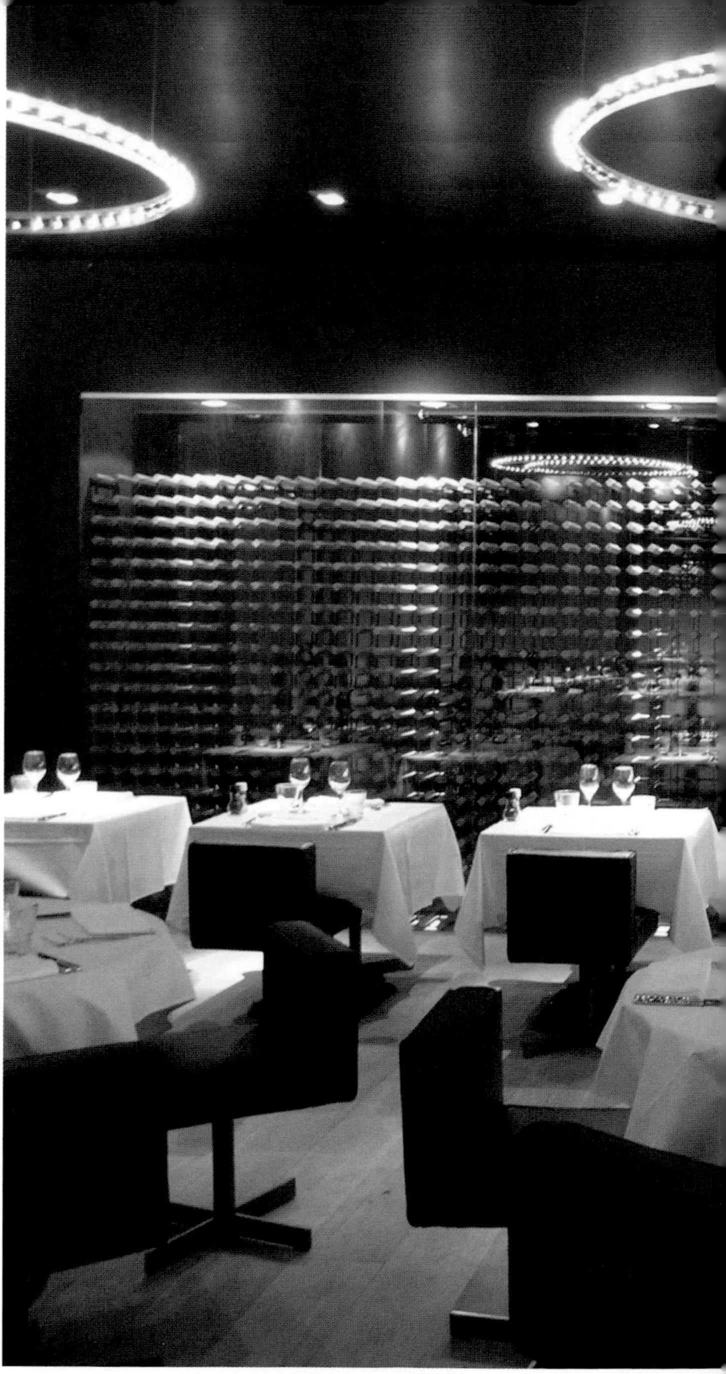

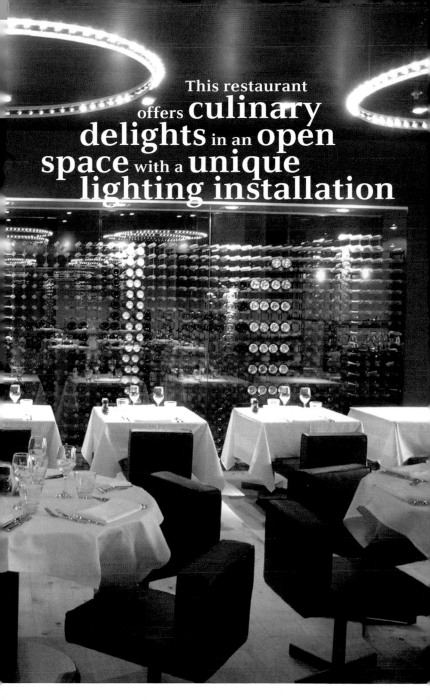

This restaurant offers **culinary delights** in an **open space** with a **unique lighting installation**

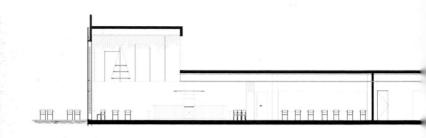

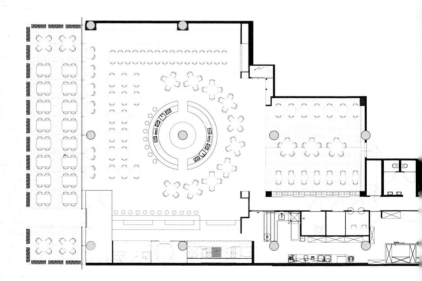

Here is **a dialogue** between **architecture** and **landscape, art** and **cuisine**

Long, extended, **plain tables** dominate the **central** dining zone

HUGO BOSS Canteen | Metzingen | RaiserLopesDesigners

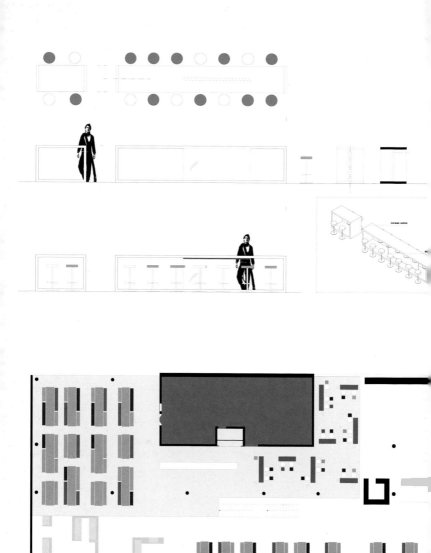

Isola Bar & Grill | Hong Kong | Leigh & Orange

Pine floors from London and the **white furnishings** create a **sun-bathed** setting

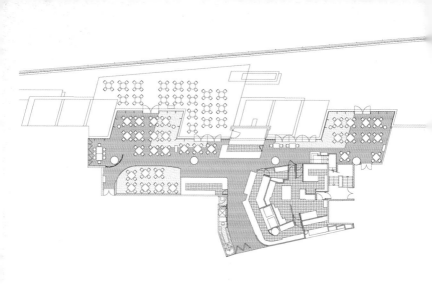

Enjoy the interaction between the solid and irregula wood tables and Tuca Reinés's photos

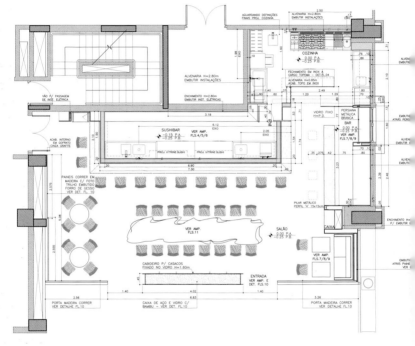

PLANTA LAYOUT
KOSUSHI DIASLU
ESCALA 1:50

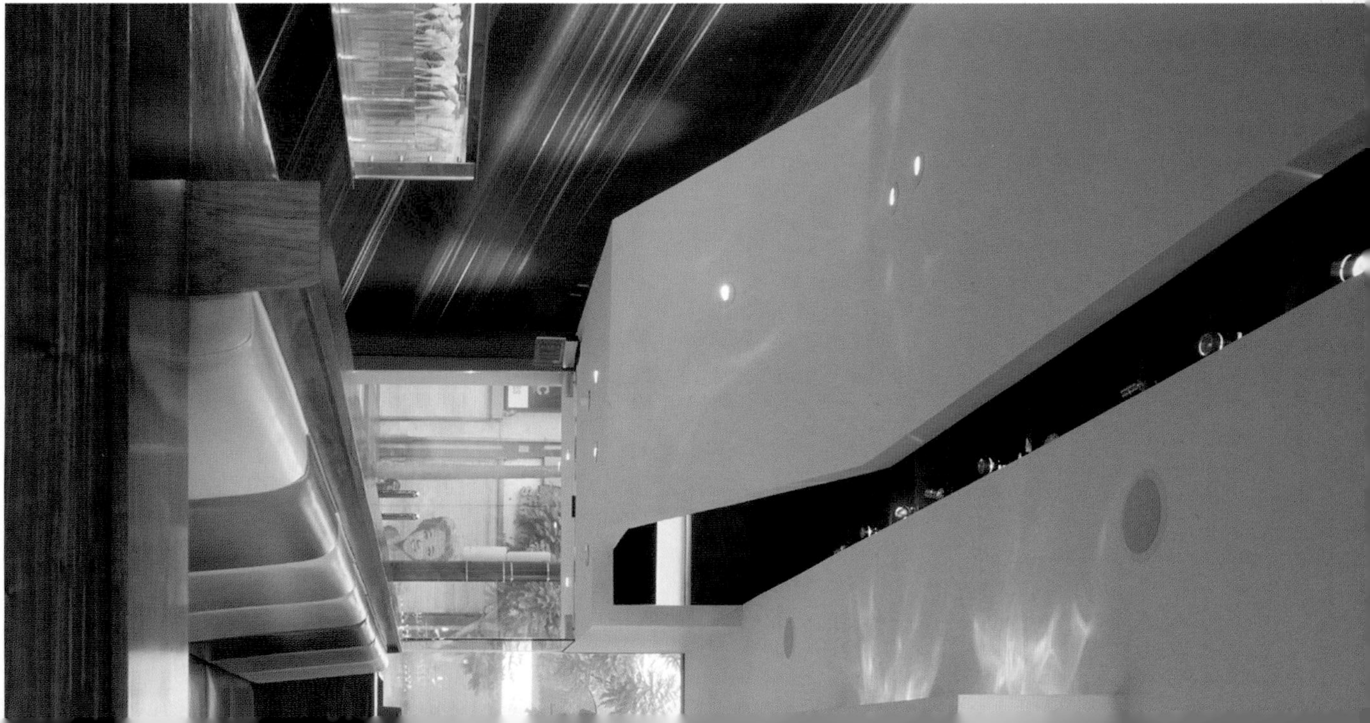

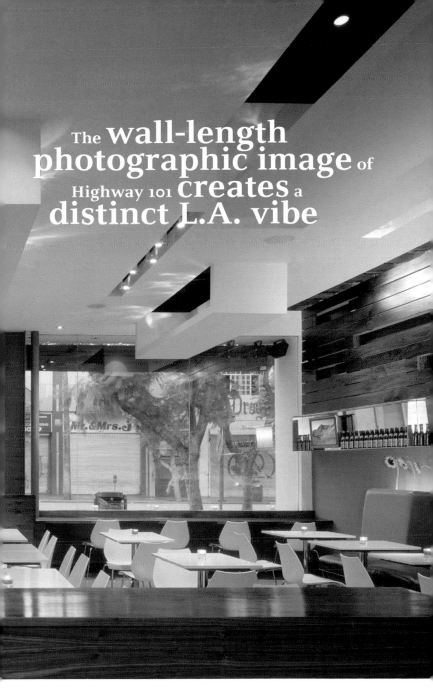

The **wall-length photographic image** of Highway 101 **creates** a distinct L.A. vibe

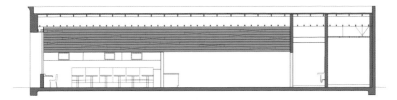

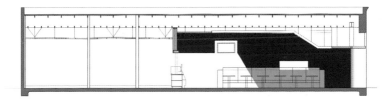

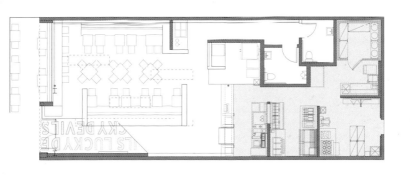

256 | **Morimoto** | Philadelphia | Karim Rashid Inc.

The **symmetrical design** features **geometric booths** with **glass** dividers

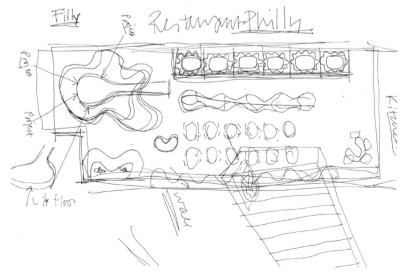

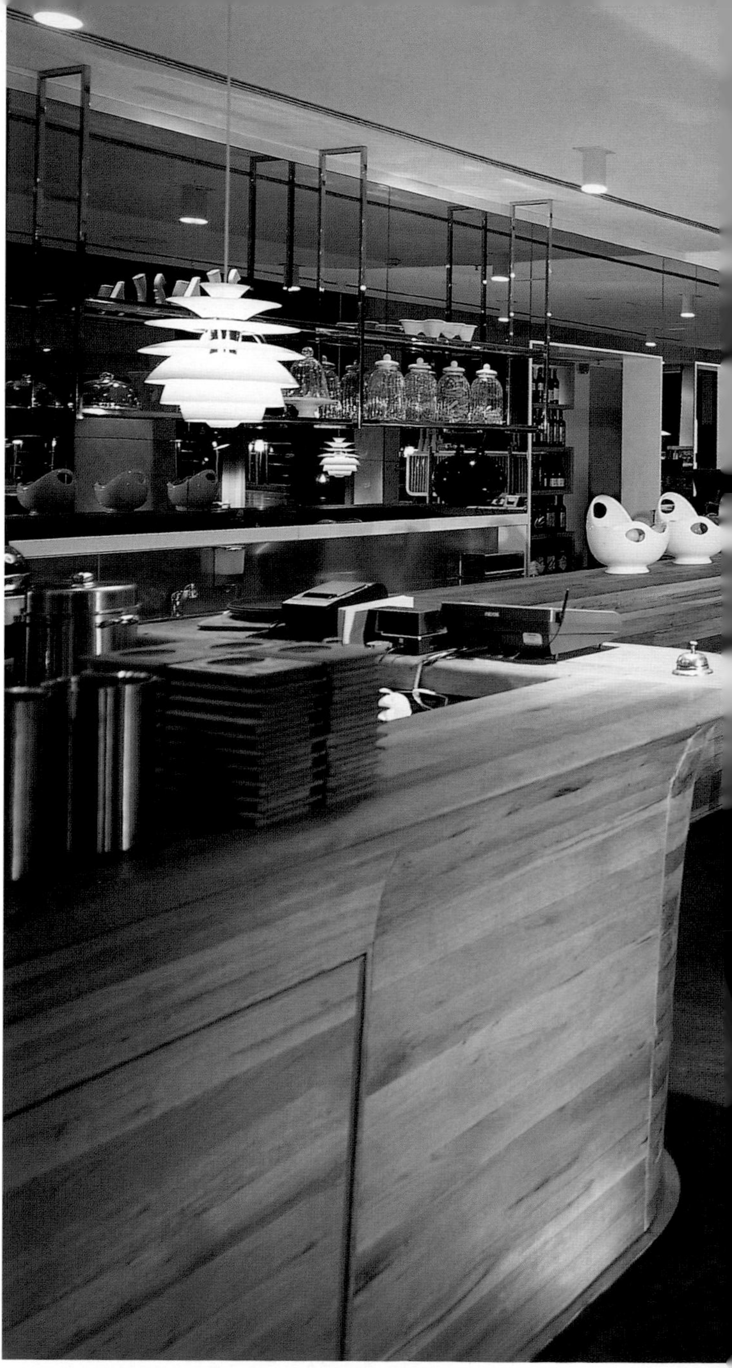

A **solid oak bar** forms the **heart** of this **establishment**

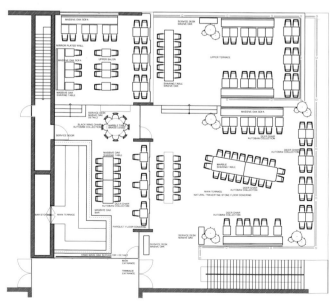

One-stop
urban-chic experience
of **wining, dining** and
dancing

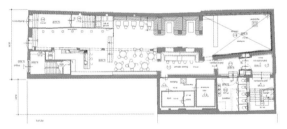

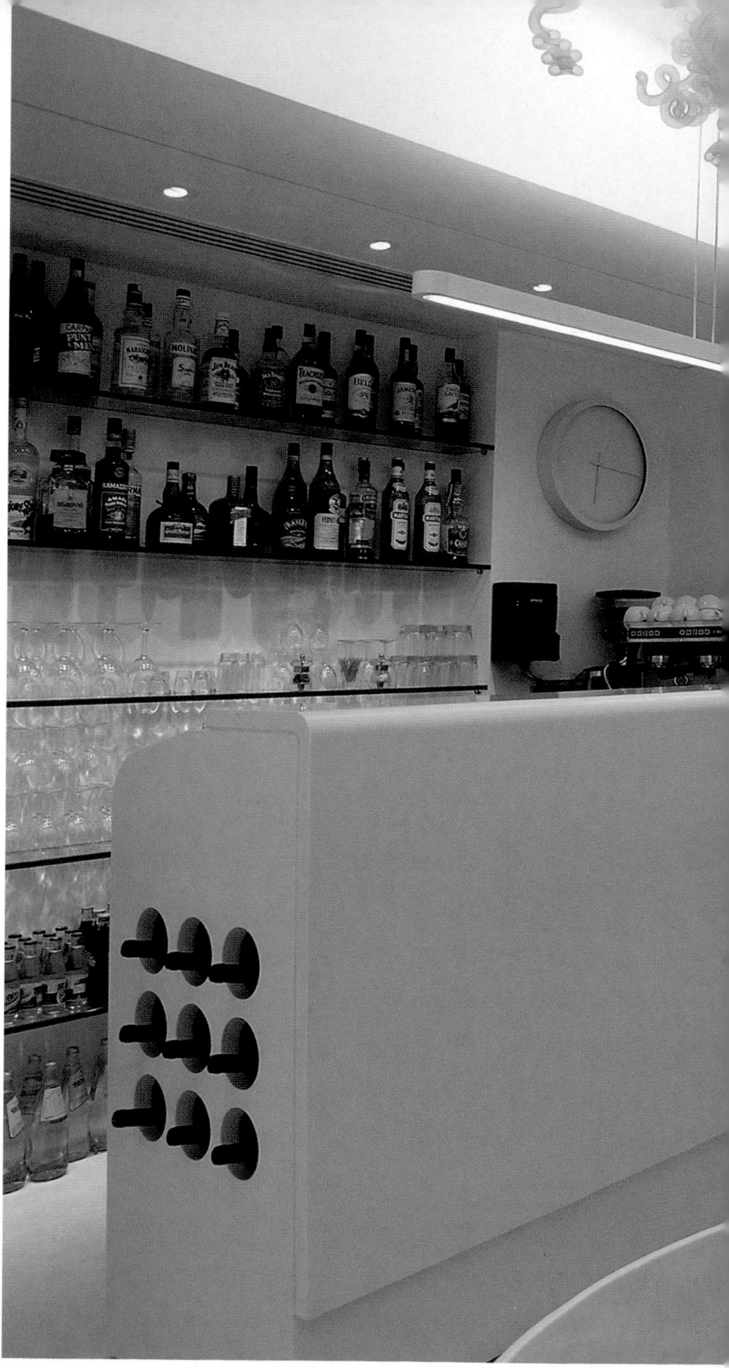

An aquarium of **delights,** this space references the **ocean throughout**

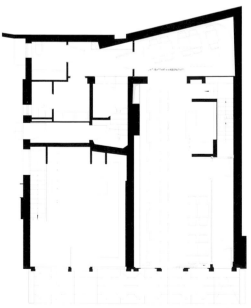

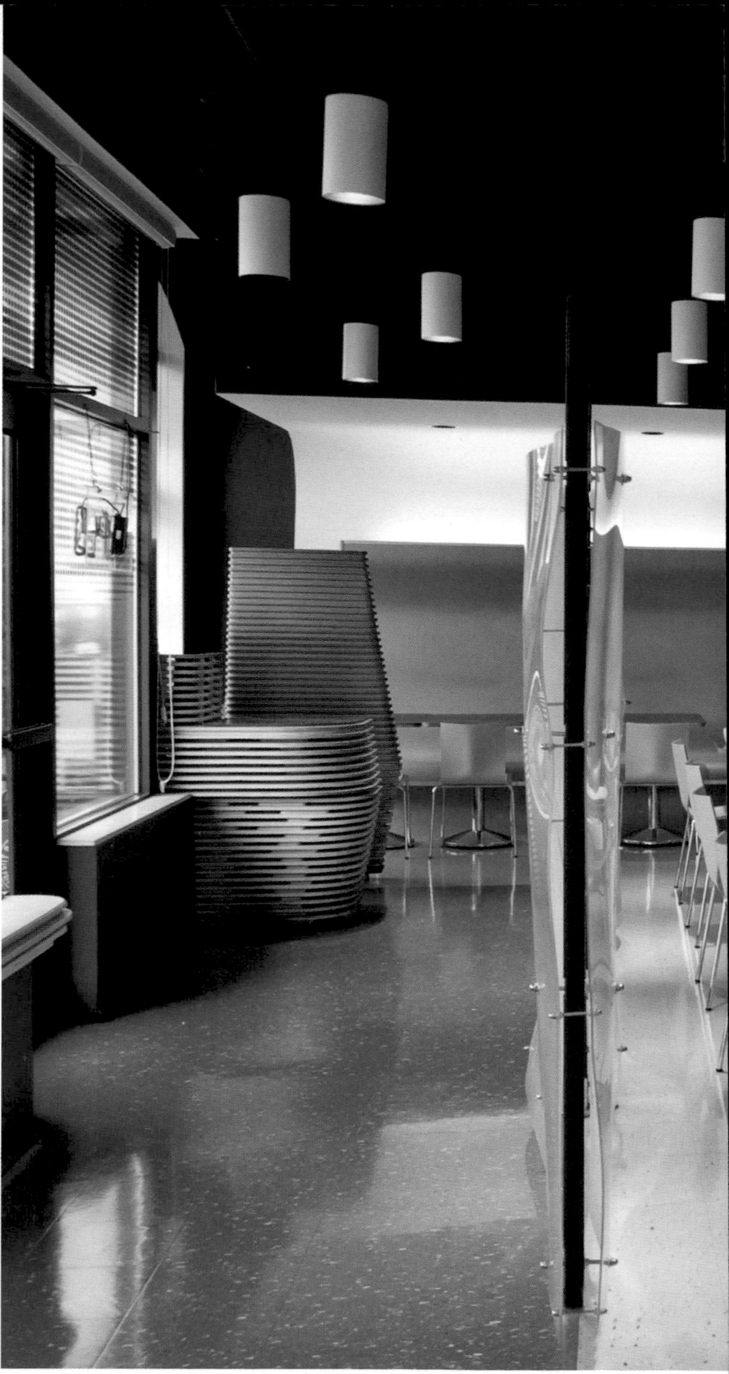

This design makes a **very clear, bold** and **graphic** statement

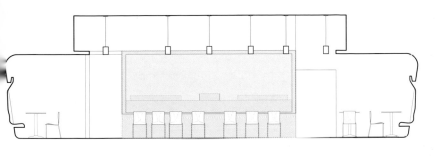

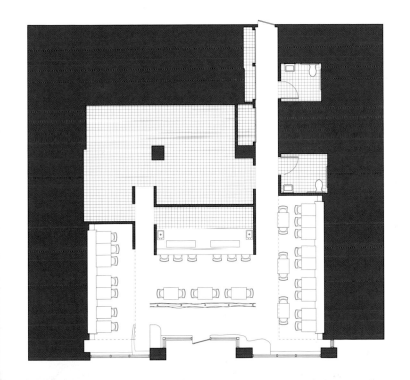

Parizzi l Parma l Costa Group and Andrea Meirana

An **unaffected use** of materials, with **little attention** to **trendy** design

Brass, oak and **strong colors** create a **relaxing** atmosphere

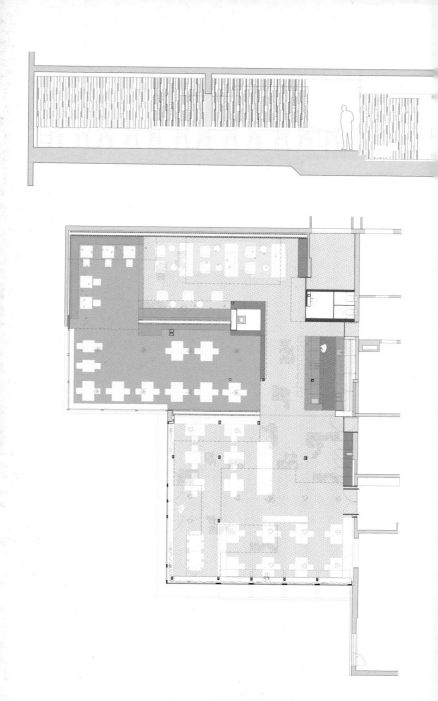

A distinguished **atmosphere** is created by **strong colors** and **unique** materials

KS

LS / GOLD / GREEN LEMON / ALK FREI   2,50

L SECCO   IN DER DOSE

OLUNDERBLÜTE / VANILLE   4,50

FFE WEIN

CHARDONNAY / MERLOT   5,90

HEISSER ZIMT-APFELSA

TASSE GLÜHWEIN

AVERNA

PIRCHER WILLIAMS

LONGDRINKS
     GIN TONIC / CUBA LIBRE / VODKA BULL

FLASCHE MARY JANE VODKA 0,2ℓ

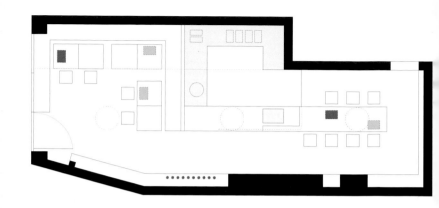

328 | **Restaurant and Bar Werd** | Zurich | Burkhalter Sumi Architects

Glossy red furniture
stands out against
a lush green floor

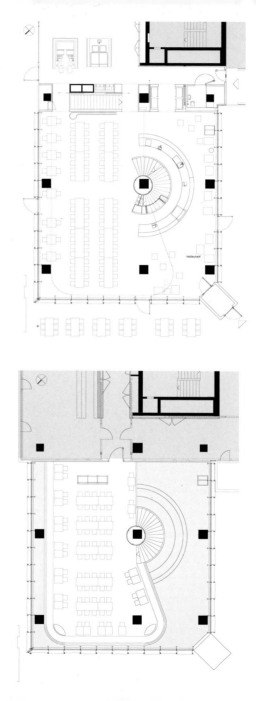

The already existent materials transform a slot space into a restaurant

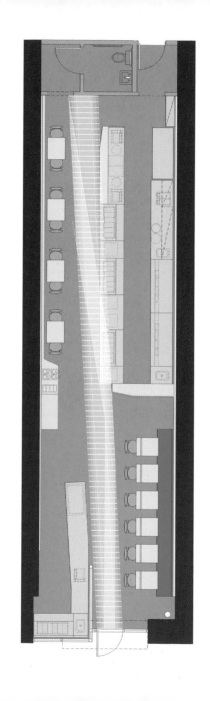

346 | **Schneeweiß** | Berlin | unit-berlin, architecture and media design

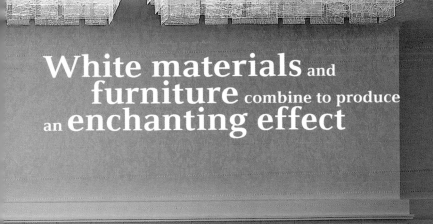

White materials and furniture combine to produce an enchanting effect

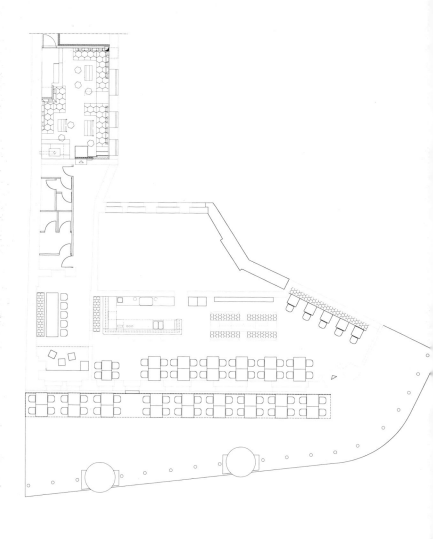

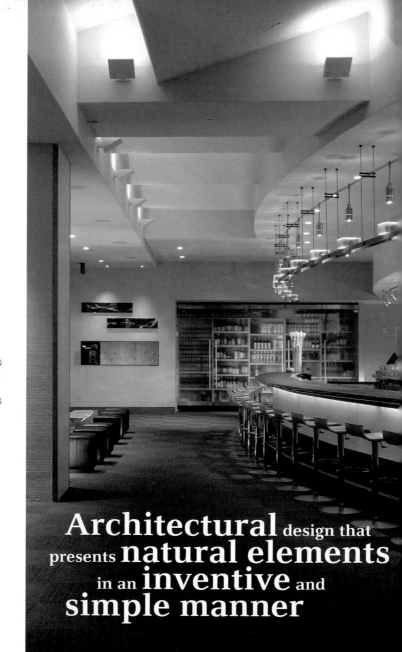

Architectural design that presents **natural elements** in an **inventive** and simple manner

The Slanted Door

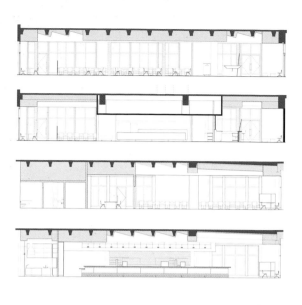

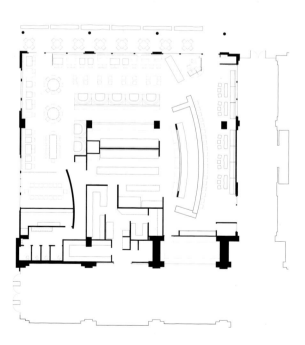

The **bourbon-toned wood, raw steel** and **cork** demonstrate a **natural elegance**

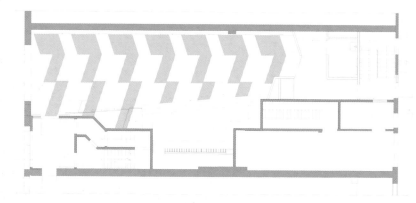

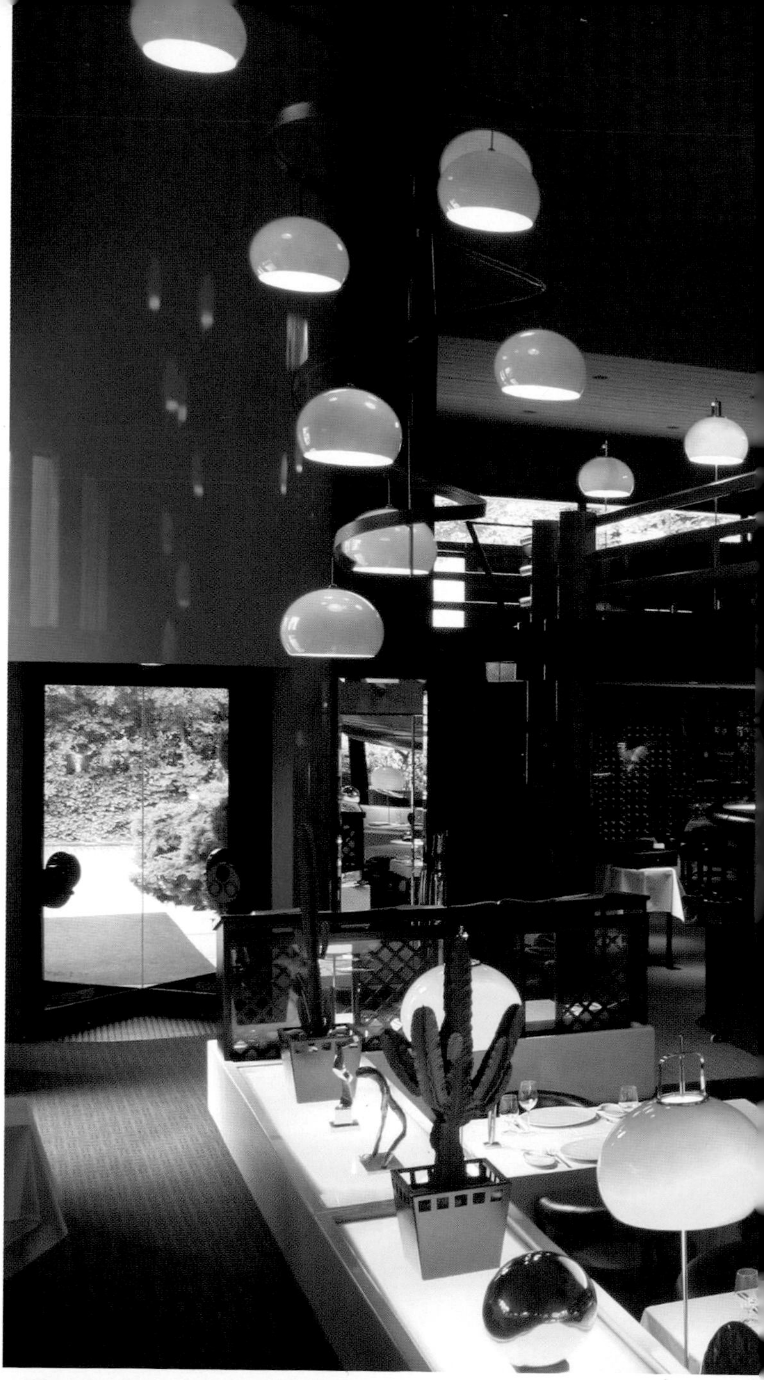

Warm colors and **harmonic proportions** give this restaurant a **perfect sense** of space

A **variety of** elements, a **modern setting** and an **eastern vibe**

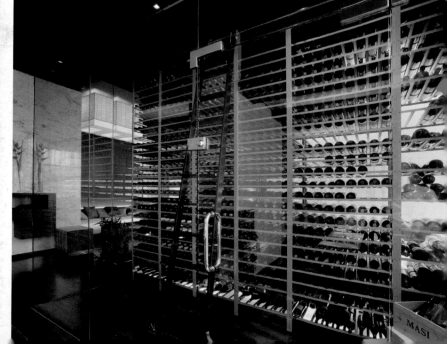

 VAU | Berlin | gmp Architekten – von Gerkan, Marg und Partner

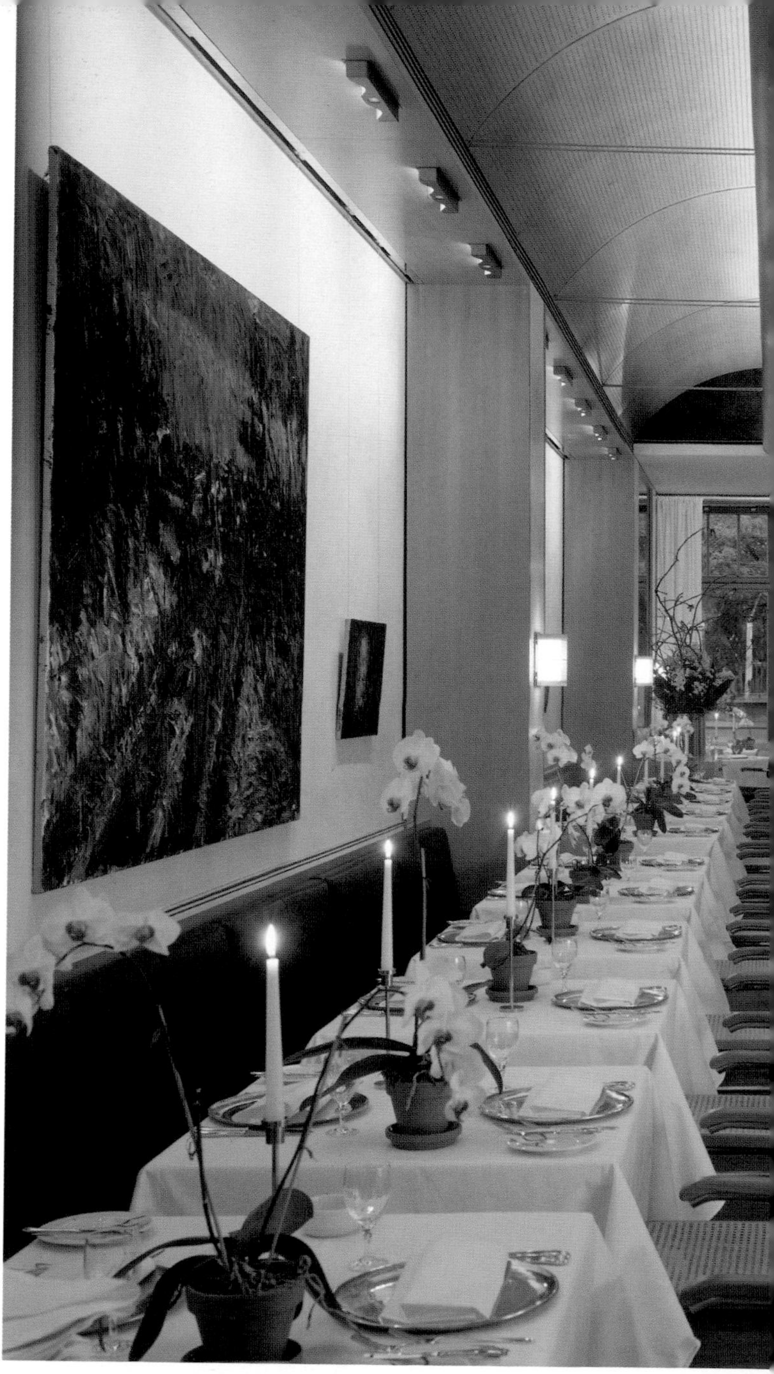

The **design** is characterized **by a combination** of **glass** and **steel, slate** and **pearwood**

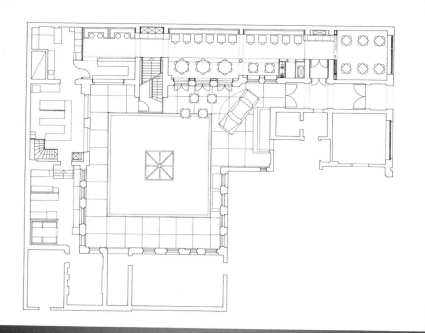

Architects Index

Picture Credits